ECHOES *of* HOPE

DEJI ATEKOJA

Echoes of Hope

Copyright © 2024 Deji Atekoja

ISBN 9798322534365

All Rights Reserved

All scriptural quotations were taken from the King James Version except otherwise stated.

Author's Contact
Email: 247relevant@gmail.com

Published by Lodeta Media & Publishing
A division of Lodeta Consulting LLC
www.lodetaconsulting.com

DEDICATION

To the loving memory of Imam Mojeed Osuolale Atekoja, who taught me to read and write English in Yoruba language.

ACKNOWLEDGEMENT

To God, that kept me and the work alive till this feat was achieved.

To Adeola Atekoja, whose unwavering support, insightful feedback, and encouragement kept me motivated throughout this journey. Thank you for believing in me and being more than a wife.

To the princesses, Emmanuela, Esther and Elizabeth Atekoja, your enthusiasm was contagious, and I am grateful for adding to the challenges that birthed this book.

To The Latter Rain Assembly, now CGCC, for the enabling environment and tutelage that inspired a great deal in shaping my mind right.

And to Damola Atekoja, who provided the notebook with which the first draft was started in 1997.

Thank you all, for your unwavering support and love. This book would not be the same without each of you.

CONTENTS

1
TAINTED CANVAS

Every newborn comes with a plain canvas
Called clean slates in many parlances
Events of life- circumstances and happenstances
Write legibly, and otherwise on it
And chiefly fueled by values of upbringing
Which many have in quantity rather than quality.

The baby becomes a child and continues
To form impressions, get persuasions and nurse intentions.
All joints supplying to orientate the pure canvas now
Tainted with indelible marked milestone memories
And imposed complexities of confusing dots of life
In dire need of guided connections in near and far future
As they endure diverse concocted critical contours
To locate the diamonds in the mud of human dispositions
Of their gory pasts, to gain the fathomed glorious future,
The prize for the price of timely correct connections
Stop dying daily, connect the dots…

◄——— NOTE ———►

A speech delivered at the in-person launch of a book titled
"Connecting the Dots," written by my wife, 'Deola Atekoja. It focuses
on the impact of upbringing as it relates to values and the need to link-
up every experience by way of leveraging on them to achieve life goals.

2
SOVEREIGNTY

Escapist? Yes, but a rational thinking
So I thought, deviating to Joppa
Desiring the cocoons of Tarshish
Rather than the abhorrent Nineveh
But contumaciously capsizing.
Oh! But for a chaotic celestial chastening:
His Immeasurable Grace overly birthed,
That pitched me in fatal aquatic splendor
Doling me a five-star lavish motel of loving hell
For even the righteous fish knew something was fishy.

The One that befriended rapacious lions to Daniel
Endeared me to a gluttonous ravening whale
To spew at the assigned prepared veiled harvest.
And dreaded like the pandemic coronavirus
I stirred utter obedient penitence in the lost.

It appeared a successful feat afterwards,
But let he that appears upright take heed:
My fed fears fiercely consumed my famished faith
Judgmentally killing who God wanted saved
And idiotically saving those He wanted dead
Till He showed me the depths of His sovereignty…
I call Him the Just One yet I could not fathom His justice.
There is one that've come to steal, kill and destroy

But He came to kill in order to make alive
So, I'm crucified with Him to live and bring to life
The captives clawed in the tender mercies of the cruel
Who can question this kind Killer?

There would be surprises at the Reckoning:
When you see the least expected
And utterly missed the much expected
Whilst wondering how you managed,
If at all.

NOTE

A poetic treatment of the rebellion of Jonah in the bible, disobeying God's commands and got swallowed by a whale while escaping to Tarshish instead of delivering God's message of deliverance to the people of Nineveh. He was spared in the belly of the fish, spewed at the place of assignment. His bane was the merciful nature of God, forgiving repentant sinners and making the declared judgement of the prophet looks like a lie. The theme was eventually weaved around the judgement day and the surprises that await everyone in heaven.

3

SOUL WINNING

A hot coming I had of it
For a journey of such faith's feat
As bars of iron went asunder
Escaping the snare of the fowler
And coming off the gate of reeds
I purposed to join the workforce of His work.

Burdened with sundry feelings
Of my sweet-bitter pasts
I forged renewed life for my hopeless hopes:
In confident assurance
Enlisted with enthusiasm,
Motivated by early comers
And questing to mend hearts
To see reasons in His seasons
Be aligned to His norms-
Deeds conforming the Creeds,
As a fruitful bough by the well
Transcending the wall
A repairer of the breach
And restorer of paths to dwell
But all to no avail!

My people were at ease in Zion
Forgetting the price of their prize

Vainly brandishing the good old days
In the face of the gory now days
Where are the fruits
With signs and wonders following?
We have bloods on our hands
Our ability to lie turns liability.
I sighed to query the hearts
As the Book says our fruits shall identify us
What is the state of our stewardship?

But for His discerning grace
When I critiqued the pulpit and the pew
It dawns I have been in Sardis
Amid illusions and detractions
Of my former illusive bosses and crew
Wrecked in uncanny deluded salvation,
Guilty by association to die avoidable death
But kept by gracious mercies of Love:
Summoning serious deepest curious courage
Becoming a skilled craftsman at His side,
And His delight day by day,
Rejoicing always in His presence.
Exceedingly fruitful and my fruits abide.

◄——— NOTE ———►

This heralds the excitement of a new convert desirous of winning souls
for God, same way he was saved, whilst working with forerunners to be
encouraged and mentored aright. He however expressed his
disappointment with how these perceived mentors discharged their
assignment with so much levity and he was getting guilty by association,
until he surrendered himself to the differentiating work of grace, that
made him exceedingly productive.

4

ARE YOU THE ONE?

I understand the Day of Reckoning by the Book
That the second Adam will return in glory
Uncannily like a thief in the night
To separate, judge, establish and reward.
Daniel and John could not preempt the fair One
But graciously He promised us signs when it draws near
Lest anyone claims situational natural ignorance
The Second has more hype than His First coming.

The Jews are back in Jerusalem amid wars and rumors
The Word wide-spread in diverse forms
Growing deceptions with ingratitude and
Novel pandemics growing untamable
As money failed, not only in Egypt.

I was quick in judging defiant Israel
But how discerning is my generation
In the face of these alarming calmness?

And I remember the sign of Jonah
Oh, strangely familiar episodes
Are you the One?

◄——— NOTE ———►

The Poet shows he's conversant with the signs and events of the end-time. He's however surprised at the gross indifference to all these by this generation despite seeing what happened, as documented in the bible by those who did same thing. In the light of recent happenings and apparent correlation with documented events and signs, he shows his apprehension and concluded asking God if it is time for the end to end.

5

KILL HIM NOW!

He stole from me
He killed my helpers
He destroyed my dreams
Heard he did to many before me
Here he stands full of boastings
He deserves to die!

But with a sigh of calming cons
The adversary is fulfilling his commission
Have you located your own to satisfy?

Spirits don't die but can be shifted!
Draw nigh for Him to draw nigh
Then you can go higher than his highest.

When I perused the characterization in the Script
To him is the role to steal, kill and destroy
But the Author and Finisher Playwright
Doles us abundant life
He casts us to cast him out:
Pursue, overtake and recover all
Validated in the Dominion Mandate of the beginning
Evidencing our victory in the battle of the seeds..

◄———— NOTE ————►

The poem is that of frustration borne out unpleasant experiences
caused the poet, especially by losing loved ones and having his dreams
shattered. He however gathered himself, after a fruitful sigh to realize
that the evil one is fulfilling his vision, he too had to face his own, as in,
the best revenge for who wants you to fail or die is to succeed or live.
His conviction and encouragement is deeply rooted in the dominion
mandate documented in the Book of Genesis and the promised victory
by God to humans over Satan after the fall in the Garden, talking about
the battle of the seeds- the Seed of Man and the seed of the devil.

6
VOICE OF A PRODIGAL

Ah! Mortgaged is my righteousness
When sequel to His acceptance
I cheaply fade into the world
Hypocritically following the cloud
With my dusk lust bringing dust
Into my completely derailed light

Or what is my fate
When my fickling faith
Relive in me the old man
Chiefly over my new man?
And when I'm simply confronted
By a protruding pair of breast bud
I turned loquacious introvert
To ponder on my dark intent.

Oh Lord! Is my failure surprising?
Let Thy Spirit convict my inspiring
Mind in the process of reconciliation
And uphold me in this course of confession.
Eliminate the fountain of these demons
To realign my amissible spirit with Yours.

Thank You Harbinger of Grace
For my journey from grass to grace

Engulfing with Your Super, my natural
And I've metamorphosized to Supernatural
While my love for You has increasingly
Change my faith and fate wholly
To be shielded eternally in Thy gate
And telling others not to be late or be late.

NOTE

This is about the realization of fallen state and loss of privileges hitherto enjoyed. The writer accepted his humanity and trust to fix him out of mercy toward becoming productive for God in the future.

7

FICKLED SAINTS

It is sorrow! Exceedingly!
That those that dwell intimately
With God's men in His grace
Have little or no impact of His?

Can we remember our faith fathers
That passed all through the seas
That were led all by His clouds
That devour all the spiritual meals
Thrown aback in the sin wilderness?

Look at Aaron-
That saw Pharoah's plagues
That saw sea parted and converged
That drank the spiritual rock
That ate the unequalled manna
Devised a new god?

Look at Gehazi-
That dwelt with virtuous God's men
That saw Naaman's rare deliverance
In a unique manner of grace
Covet pecuniary gains?

Even Judas Iscariot-
That saw the Light at work
Personally worked miracles
Drank His blood and ate His body
Not only loot His treasury
But handed Him over
(Though to be glorified)

Oh! What a grace-grass move
A conspiracy of the Jewish saints
That fixed the Gentile on hold
Are we holding on to the Light?

NOTE

A straightforward rebuke for saints of God, who having been serving
in His vineyard return to their vomits, to be involved with things they
earlier condemned. Biblical allusions were made, and the conclusion is a
strong charge for those still on course and ready to hear, to continue
steadfastly in the Father's love.

8
LET HIM

Singing the blues is pitiable,
Demanding response beyond ethics
I tell you, inherently inevitable,
Lest you sink further, struggling
To come out of life's miry clay
And succumb to a serene sighing state
Like one in tonic immobility with no delay.

Why me? Is out of the question!
If not you, who?
It should and must be you
If you'll let Wisdom reign without portion.

I remember the plight of Job
Indeed, "happy is the person
Whom God corrects!
Do not resent it when He rebukes you."
Take it as a time to sigh, consider your stock
And stick to your God that keeps covenant and mercy
For them that love and wholly observe His charges.

If He let Himself to be born poor in a manger
If He let Himself to get taunted by the evil ones
If He let His prophet walked naked and
If He let His man marry a harlot to prove a point

If He did not spare Moses, David and Israel
Who you be? Why these emotive prayers?
My life's sojourn has taught me He's terrible,
He's sovereign, killing without committing murder
And His silence, a veritable answer
For God loathes stupid litanies.
If you can't trace Him, Trust Him.

NOTE

An identification of possible downtimes is noted here, where reasons
abound to be dejected and sorrowful. The poet exemplified the
harrowing effects of this and makes some biblical allusions in that
regard, while enjoining everyone in such a state not to take it personal
or as something unique or specially targeted at them. It ends with a
clarification of God's sovereignty, just nature and the need to be always
wholly dependent on Him.

9

NOSTALGIA

Vividly I can still flash back to
The joy of that august day
When my ignoble life slain
The old man and his traits
With the lamb on the cross
Sequel to His glorious rise
And I starved myself of those
Worldly entreaties with ease.

But what did I meet
When later His mind fled
When focus melted and faded
And the old man engulfed
With soothing worldly joys
I turned to a sound hypocrite
Cherishing Ceaser and God
And my mouth a watered fire.

Descended on me now is a chaotic dominion
Ye! Honestly now I've discerned
Your insuperable peace proffered
Which You mete not at world's ilk
Adduced I now is the bitter truth
God cannot be fooled.

◄——— NOTE ———►

This is a direct comparison of two phases of life: The joy of salvation, when the writer just surrendered his life to God and how he became the exact opposite on a disgraceful low. It however ended well for him as he was able to retract back under the weight of God's dominion with a conclusion on God's Omniscience, "God cannot be fooled."

10

PARADIGM SHIFT

Listen Assemblages of God's disciples
You're the church not the monument
Temples of God are a movement
With the sole business to witness

Listen angels of God to the churches
Superstars! Why are you still folded
With spiritual opulence while the sheep's
Inundated plagues daily mounted?

It's high time for power to be shifted
From the pulpit to the pew,
With a paradigm devised
To decentralize power by the few

Arise! O ye saints,
Be the new breed without greed,
A radical opposition to hocus pocus
Whose deeds correlate the creed.

Church! A great commitment
To the great commandment
And the great commission
Fuels fulfillment of the great mission.

So desire and decide with determination
To earnestly embrace the gospel
Like the Apostles showing in action
That God's temples may be a living epistle.

◄——— NOTE ———►

Inspired by the Book of Revelations, the writer gave a direct warning to religious leaders and congregations on allowing the free gifts of God to operate freely. It tries to redefine church as a movement, people of God trusting and doing His will, and not the structural building. He therefore urged all to uphold the Great Commission with conscious desire, convincing decision, and unflinching determination to dominate their environment, by making their lives a living epistle for people around to read to the honour of God.

11
LIVING IN TRUST SONG

Only name to be praised
Is the name of the Lord
He's marvelous, He's wonderful
Praise! The name of the Lord

From the rising of the sun
To the setting of the same
Let us praise! The name of the Lord.

Only name to be praised
Is the name of the Lord
He's marvelous, He's wonderful
Praise! The name of the Lord

Somebody shout Hallelujah
Somebody shout praise the Lord
Praise the Lord, O ye people
Praise! The name of the Lord

Let's praise Him in understanding
Let's praise Him in the Spirit
Let's praise Him when we can't trace Him
Let us praise! The name of the Lord

ⱶ———— **NOTE** ————ⱶ

It is a verse aimed at giving praise to God for His marvelous nature and deeds. It did not just urged people to praise God, but also prescribed that this be always done in understanding and in Spirit, that even when it seems we cannot see God in the situations of our lives, we should continue to trust Him.

12

HEEDING THE CALL SONG

I'll move Lord Almighty I'll move
From my soothing comfort I'll move
Where I pitch my tent I'll move
For now I'm strengthened I'll move
Never to be hindered I'll move
To follow the cloud of grace I'll move
Now is the time Lord to build and build
I'll move Lord I'll move.

◄——— NOTE ———►

This is a conviction-based song, where the writer pledges to leave his
comfort zones and go all the way with God. This is premised on the
understanding that there is no better time than now.

13

WHAT SAYS THE CLOCK?

Father Beek, father Beek
Come in haste to tell
Come to tell a tale
From the work of clock

Tick tick tick
Always says the clock
Quick quick quick
In all forms of work

Good good good
In all work we do?
Quick quick quick
We shall see to that.

This is a rhyme for kids to learn about timeliness, especially as it
pertains to speed and accuracy. It has no religious undertone, but just
simple counsel.

14
OBEDIENCE

God told Noah
To build Ark
Noah then did all that God said
And God spared his family.

Therefore children
Listen to God
Do His will now everyday
He will spare your family.

This is a bible-based rhyme for children about obedience. It heralds the story of Noah's obedience and the benefits, concluding on the need for children to emulate him and that the benefits, like Noah's, transcends them, but would extend to their family.

15
TURNING POINT

Never again will it occur
That I'll ever manipulate Him
No! Faded is the urge
From within and without me.

Pourquoi?
It's dawn on me here and now
That to experience the full
Manifestation of His glory,
Not only should He be
My Christ and Saviour
But Lord over all
That concerns my being
In all ramifications

What about the clique?
Tell them I retire for I'm tired
To be privy to the parley
Of Heresies and Apostasy
Hindering His reign in the terrain
For it's not my will but His
Not my way but His
God! Cannot be fooled.

◄——— NOTE ———►

This is a reflection of a prodigal, whose recent experience has taught never to go on the route of disobedience again. The decision is fortified by his readiness to denounce every relationship and sins that easily beset him because "God cannot be fooled."

16
WINDOWS OF HEAVEN

Windows of heaven are opened
Why are you suddenly fulfilled
Over this fickling wealth?
Do you think this is God's best
That you seem so ignorantly content?
You hoard and worship your endowments
Know you not that no one receives
Except that given from above?

Ah! Obey God and live as you should
Hinder not His hearty purpose
Or you experience the plague of Vashti-
Elimination by substitution.
Despise not His divine imperative
To have your valley of Achor
Turned into a door of hope
Even as your tithes protects against the devourer
And your integrity positions you for favour
Leaving your offering to financially increase you.

Let the haughty remember the Potentiate
That satiated the wants of Day Seven
Accordingly in the initial six days
God owns it all, plus you.

◄──── NOTE ────►

With a strong allusion to the counsel of God to Abraham to "live as he should," in order to get the promised blessings of God, the poet admonishes the reader to be focused on God's almightiness, especially ability to provide for our needs, rather than being haughty, greedy or be distracted by transient wealth. He believes honouring God with our belongings will prevent them from experiencing things like loss of position (like Vashti, a queen who was replaced for being too proud to honour the king) or remaining permanently in an inglorious position.

In conclusion, he specifically identified the benefits of tithing (protection from devourer), integrity (favour) and offerings (strategic financial positioning). The last word is a very strong warning to the haughty to remember God as the only potentiate, who owns everything and everyone.

17

THE BURDEN OF HIS WORD

"In the beginning was the Word,
And the Word was with God,
And the Word was God."
Beyond the comprehension of the speed of light
Piercing above the tsunamic intensity known to man
The Word hits man's trinity: spirit, soul and body
The blood, water and flesh to all sinews, not spared
And all hitherto beliefs melted into thin air
To confirm our deceived hopes were mere pan's flash,
But the timing of manifestation is His prerogative.

Are you indeed a prisoner of hope?
It's a thing to have hope in the future
It's another to have future in the hope
The fountain of your hope
Predicates its success and tenor
Be careful what you hear and how you hear
     "He that pays the piper dictates the tune"
     If your dream is God-given
     Let your deeds be God-driven

     He says to one "take up your bed and walk"
     To another, "go, wash in the pool Siloam"

Even to his dear friend, he delayed four days.
Till the brightness of his light dimmed out

Has your word ever been harsh on Him
Has it ever challenged His prowess to fix your issues
Have you cried "Lord! This is not what you showed me?

Hold on to the Light
His Word to you often time is unique to you
Like the lonely, windy and dusty path of destiny
If you cannot trace Him, trust Him
That knows the way through the wilderness
That is the apparel of His unfailing veiled Word.
Radiates around till the set time, never returns void to Him.
Desire, decide and determine to dominate while you wait-
Assuredly, there shall be a performance.

◄——— NOTE ———►

This is an encouragement to the discouraged not to lose hope, by
emphasising the dynamic ways in which God relates with different
people in turning their sorrows to joy. The conclusion is therefore for
the hopeless to become hopeful, holding on to the promises of God,
that there shall always be a performance of His word.

18
THE TONGUE

When the human tongue I appraised
I saw there-in precisely the rudder
In its minute formation
Issuing to the ship great orders
That made me mad with fascination
And my buccal agape in alalia:
A small organ that speaks big
To wreck in the ilk of fire
In its world of wickedness.

Among the body's members
Stand out ye at a vantage
Though not in phenotype
To taint the body all around.

If not in thy lack lack I words
A good wish the relief could've been
As your words are eggs
An irredeemable outburst
That make or mar the donor
With a little or no control kit.

You mete different rewards for lone usage:
The tongue which harvests applause
Can reap reproach in future near

Can you ever be tamed
As animals in circus?

Oh! You're the sweetest bitter organ
If I make no mistake with you
Undoubtedly a perfect man I'd be
Able in the state to tame the whole body
Whenever at ilkaday

And when I remember that I change not
My tongue to change my tongue
I'm changed from my ignorant indifference
To bring my obeisance to the powerful human tongue

NOTE

The poem opens with a comparison of the tongue with a rudder, used
to pilot ships. The main idea and comparison are the overall
importance of the two to the rest of the body parts. It concludes with
an ode to the tongue, wondering wether this human part can be tamed.

19

YOU ARE HERE TO RULE

Right from the very first glimpse of this world
Be it in unsavory mangers or scrumptious crib's craic
Are the cries of discomfort enthralling all but the baby
Querying the eviction from the womb's soothing hedges.
You're not privy to the choice of parenthood:
Be it sperm donors or accidental discharges
Ready, unplanned or imposed parenthood
As in our degenerate-world of babies birthing babies
You had no say in the choice of birth-place:
Be it in the palace or the dunghill of the
Developed, developing or underdeveloped nations!

Welcome to the human race
The uncanny denominator
Is that all that predicate our coming?
Is His eternal purposes in oblivion?

You're His image and assuredly not deleterious accident
A diligent crafting of varying empowering constituents
The matter's meat is the quantum of productivity
Adequately enabling a recoup
Of His unmatchable Investments?
And you know
Sequel to Responsibilities are Reports and Rewards
Good or bad, every Report on given Responsibilities

Attracts a Reward. Go on the path
To Desire, Decide, Determine and Dominate
"Thy Kingdom come is a call to battle even in the rattle for
Replenish the earth, Subdue it and Have Dominion
Is an Invitation to Rule!

NOTE

The inability of anyone to choose their parents or place of birth is the
first point of call here. This is linked to the eventual display of
discomfort expressed by newborns as a response to a change of
environment at birth, while in most cases, the parents and others
rejoice. The writer then moves on to address the issue of racism,
stating that the only race is the human race, regardless of colour, which
is "uncanny denominator" for all. He believes that everyone is created
with serious attention paid to details by God (not by accident), who
also has a purpose for each and everyone. Concluding, he hinted
pastorally on the dominion mandate as the purpose of being counted
among the human race.

20

PRAYER TECHNOLOGY

Oh terribly great gracious God
Thou covenant keeping Dad
For those that will an obey
Diligently Your will without delay
O Lord of hosts, God of Israel
Heaven and earth is Thy toil

Incline Your ears to me Lord
And open thy eyes I beseeched
To see the plagues and reproach
Of the world in my very reach
Professing in their foolish mind
How short Your hand is to rescue Dad

Lord! my sins before Thee tabled
Your roles descried I played
Your faithfulness discerned standout
Oh my iniquities drove to this path
Where I languish endlessly sad
Like one without faith, grace and Dad.

Oh Lord I remember your quest
That if I transgress, I'll adustly disject
But whenever I change to Thy will
And keep Thy commandments will

I be gathered to be well conformed
To fulfil that which I am designed.

Lord remember Thy love's magnitude
Through Thy only Son that for my sake
Died and rose for me to rise
And bounce back into Thy love.
Thank you, Father, for this plague
Is no match for past and this grace.

— NOTE —

The mainstay here, as suggested by the title is an observed pattern of praise and thanksgiving before making requests when Christians pray. The sequence is borne out of a pattern documented in Nehemiah 9, where God is presented as commensurate with His reward. When you obey Him, you get a good reward and when otherwise, you still have a just recompense. The conclusion is on the finished work of redemption on the cross, wherein God shows His enduring love towards all mankind.

21
JETTISONED

The commission conceived from cradle,
A premonition for the days of turmoil
When the demands of manly establishment
Will raise their nature-orchestrated faces in phases:
I thought of it in a way somewhat easy
With prejudice to the constant changing change
Whose gory engulfs our national glory.

Like a quiet storm to onlookers within and without
Haughtily following intuitive perfect plans.
Doomed! It succumbs to the weight of winding ways
A sequel to the fragrance of our national character
Suffering and smiling in agonizing slender joy…
Forgetting famous flicking faces of evil.
Naija decides our future, not our plans.

Now I know we're perpetually programmed to fail
In the hands of the worst of us ruling the rest of us
While the best of us continues to major in minors.

And young men get disoriented, JAPA abroad
While grown ones throw hopes aboard
Ours is a nation of planned accidents
Good or bad.

◄──── **NOTE** ────►

It is commonly believed that planning is good for predictable success. The poet, however, shows the impact of the environment on the success or otherwise, of the plan. Using Nigeria as the setting, it portrays one who started planning early but had all plans shattered by the constant change, usually from bad to worse that characterizes the country. He expressed his frustration in "now I know we're perpetually programmed to fail..." The conclusion is on the effects of this unfavourable environment leading to brain drain and hopelessness, due to the prevailing "planned accidents."

22
ARROW SHOT INTO THE FUTURE

Yesterday,
I rode innocently into the world
To a standing ovation led by a debutant mother
That turned a flat-pan's flash in time
As I faced the angry music
Of my juvenile beats
In mother's regimented tutelage.

Today,
I reap the fruit of her toil
And realize for certain the good
Her incessant cruel commands
Donated coercively to my enviable state.

Tomorrow,
As I bliss-swim sequel to my Today
In my mountainous merry mansions
Reciprocating in extravagant excess
Her invaluable clairvoyant foresights
An investment of dutiful maternal love
Better let it be!
If you don't know my story
Do not despise my glory

◄──── NOTE ────►

The poet here sees himself as one on a mission, a mission that started with a determined mother instilling great discipline early in him. This investment pays good dividends as he continues to make headway in life and urged no one to stand on his way, as he purposed to repay his mother with all manners of appreciation.

23

ENEMY WITHIN

I sat down again, sighing
The inner voice said solemnly
"You've got to your stress' ceiling"
And my heart's eyes opened
"I know your gut's feelings…
It's also your strength signal,"
I rose into more confusion
Pondering how this formidable barrier
Is pointing to my strength?
"Assuredly, pathway to your vision fulfillment."
And the voice left.

Evaluating my mental laziness
And trading my forlorn fate for faith
I inferred the specified strength signal
Lies inherent in awakening my inner fortitude
And developing my skills set
In the light of my expectation.

What's even my expectation?
I realized I needed one
I need a destination birthed by purpose.
So, I sat seeking strategic steps
Set aside every weight
That easily besets the consistency
Needed for my vision assignment.

And I got fueled by a confident hope
For the joy that was set ahead
To birth both the will and ability
And silencing my self-consciousness
With stoppage to rationalization for failure
Which I called self-sabotage
I gained clarity, connecting the dots
I'm a miracle going somewhere to happen

NOTE

The poem is a dialogue between the writer, at his wits end, and his inner voice, with the latter admonishing him about his frustration with life. He learnt about the pros and cons of one reaching his stress ceiling as well as the appropriate ways to deal with it. The poet eventually took the counsels and was able to leverage on a seeming bad situation to get propelled by hope, having received insights. He connected the necessary dots of his life and became so expectant of a better tomorrow.

24

THINKING BIG

Success plans and purposes are too big
To be encapsulated in a soul
That's why success void of succession
Tantamount failure, and full of regrets
The One that sharpened the edges of hearts
Is transgenerational in all dispositions
Look in the Book for empirical attestations

Thinking big is righteous
So says the Alpha and Omega
That thinks it, sees it and says it into existence
He always gets at the end what
He wanted in the beginning
Like Abraham saw in the similitude of the stars
That changed his perception of the blessing

"I can do it" speaks to a good idea
A God-idea is not literally so
"It's within reach" speaks to a good idea
A God-idea is not literally so
It puts your problems in perspective and
Says to them "you are not as big as you seem!"

A God-idea is a big and compelling vision
A God-idea can only be done through God

A God-idea drives for succession
A God-idea always compels team building
A God-idea produces a hundred-fold perpetually.

Think big! Build a system
Initiate a tactical job operation
And remove bottlenecks…

It helps you to prioritize
It draws you closer to Purpose
It draws you closer to like-minded persons
And repels those that think you're a mental health patient
It will force you to collaborate, interdependence!
It will awaken the giant within you, competition!
It will activate time-wasting detectors, effectiveness!
Thinking big is a win win all the time.

Give your life a meaning, purpose-driven!
Give yourself reasons to grow, personal development!
Give yourself a reason to take the lead
Dream of your destiny, despite need for endurance:
Pleasure from junk foods births disliked-obesity
Pain from workouts births loved-fitness
You're destined to impart
You're empowered for impact
You're being blessed to become a blessing
A conduit for answering certain prayers
You're where you are for such a time as this.
That is your given enablement
The best ability is God's ability.

◄———— NOTE ————►

The poem is about having great expectations from life, such that transcends even the person. The importance of succession is therefore hinged upon, as alluded in the biblical accounts of Abraham in respect of God's promise to him. He also did a definition of 'a good idea' versus 'a God-idea', respectively viewed as what we can do by ourselves and what only God can help us with. The poet concludes with the need to build a working system to execute the big plan, which helps to prioritize, understand purpose, and build relationships, among others.

25

DOWNING THE DUCK

They call him a Duck
That is foolish in his brand of wisdom
That will rather be critical than correct
And Orders become water on a duck's back
Gullibly vulnerable to flipping friendly foes
With Tools disguised to Crack his Ignoble Shell
Why would you be a duck?

They call him the Duck
That sees his determined deviance as little sin
And being rubbed with gearing grooming grease
Of manipulative molds of wolves in sheep's clothing
Developing the duck patiently for the Turnout's harvest
They duly duck him that is ready to buck the Book
Why would you be the duck?

He is truly an irredeemable duck
That could leverage the chance to retrace his steps
Sequel to a lightened darkness of his colorless guilt
But confronted by a choice between two evils
Escorted the corpse like the uncanny fly
To the grave-point of no return
And the duck becomes a Golden Goose.

Now the day of reckoning beckons
The Duck docked craning like fish out of water
Lacking supposed supporting spine of Policy and Morality
Tossed around by the imminent dawning destined doom
"Quack! Quack"! The duck's bent, battered and booed
For the ruler of Law will always expose crooked lines
And when the Ruler of corrections comes...
What kind of officer would be found in YOU:
Officer Being-Straight, practicing the truth-
Officer Staying-Straight, self-developing and leveraging-
Officer Living-Straight, setting goals and working it?
There is no fence to sit on
Nature abhors vacuum.

◄———— NOTE ————►

The poem is a strong warning for everyone in position of authority to beware of people's false humility, closeness, or relationships, as many are surreptitiously laced with ulterior motives capable of implicating the unsuspecting officer. The mainstay of the work is for readers to ensure they discharge their official capacity by the book, as a safeguard for any form of query. Like a double-edged sword, the poet weaved this into man's keeping all of God's commands to excel on the judgement day.

26
ODE TO DEATH

Thou art but eternal bereavement
Designed, undesirable divine development
Gushing gluttonous and respecter of nobody
Oh, carnivorous craftsman of joy's slender body
Why don't you ever give up
To disman human cells when we're up
Or spare us not when we're down
But set-up this dogged daggers-drawn?

How I seldom wonder what you are
Unquestionable by our arrogant quizzes here
As we all say yes to your conquering caprices
Oh, leveler and sjambok for friends and foes.

With you there is no rich, poor or betwixt
Uncertain and fair with no prejudice.
Who am I to contemplate a question
When you consume those in position
Devouring the divinely and devilishly gold rich?
Where can I sojourn to evade thy reach?

Tutelage by thoughts, experiences, and inferences
Learnt truly we're no match for your preference
So, thy militant mercy I solicit
To rejoice at my transient sit

Indeed, I salute your knocking knack
Of not being in any clique
Meting and doling your wroath
To the affluent and gutter blood at equal length.

I write because you have not touched me
But have seen your mercurial hands on my liefs
Spared not due to anything found in me
But His enduring merciful grace that saves,
That brought life and immortality to light in the Book:
Death has been abolished!

NOTE

Simply an address to 'death'. It hints on the unbiased nature of how
death kills, regardless of gender or social status. The poet dwelt so
much on the seeming high influence death has on human judging by its
operational capacity. It did not take for granted that he was even able to
write the poem because death hasn't come his way, a grace he attributed
to the saving hands of God.

27

THE DEARTH OF TRUTH

Know now that the events confirm the dearth!
As our self-seeking acts conform the ignoble dirt
That, wherein we dwell, killed truth to death
With impunity, enthralling falsehood over truth
Sowing bad seeds and praying for crop failure with
Roaring applause for fallen values with streets' strength,
Men prefer faking it to making it
Continually providing platforms for lies
Abandoning the Way, the Truth and the Life!

Who taught the newborn the first lie?
Sequel to externalities of desperately wicked hearts
Harboring lies of varying species and packages
Just to eat and have the undeserved cake?
Cry... Beloved Country
It is a world of The Concubines
In the quest for Infinite Riches
Chike missed the ferry and commingled with robbers
In A Season of Migration to the North saying it's
A Question of Power as The Arrow of God falls on us
For The Man Died at The Famished Road
Since The Beautiful Ones Are Not Yet Born,
Things Fall Apart and Brother Jero is not tried
Even those born Without a Silver Spoon are entangled
In the Blood Knot by Nervous Conditions

To exit the House of Hunger and Dry White Season
The Joy of Motherhood seized with Women at Point Zero
Such that even Eze could not go to School and
It's now a Dangerous Love for Agbo to Live in Calabar…

A lucid preposterous mix holds sway:
The gods are not to be blamed for
Falsehood from pulpit to the pew
Insincerity from pew to the pulpit
Amid deft political abracadabras
Of bloody booming Blood Banks
And gravely Gold Dreams…
And my people love it so!

◄——— NOTE ———►

The work attempts to query the prevalence of falsehood, "…killed
truth to death with impunity," unfortunately followed by indifferent
hypocrisy of "…faking it to make it," "…sowing bad seeds and praying
for crop failure" with "…applause for fallen values with street's
strength". Evaluating the problem further, the poet tried to trace the
source of the problem before beautifully paying tribute to some
African works of art just to add credence to the poem's thematic
preoccupation. Back to where it started, the poem ends with how much
falsehood is condoned, "…and my people love it so."

28

LIMERICK OF A CAT

Boast not your big size beyond your boarders!
Lest you meet one bigger and catly perilous.
Surreptitiously humble your feat,
Lest you're taken off your seat.
Hope you'll heed my free friendly counsels?

— NOTE —

As the title suggests, it's a limerick, short verse of three long and two
short lines, rhyming 'aabba'. Here, it is all about a cat being counseled
to be weary of haughtiness, as he may just encounter one more "catly"
than him.

29

THE ROAD TO YESTERDAY

Today is the Tomorrow of Yesterday:
Yesterday is gone
Today is going
Tomorrow is ever here!
Why hinged on uncontrollable Yesterday
Rather than process the privileged Today:
A surety for a better Tomorrow and
A foolproof of learning from history.

The path to Yesterday is shameful regrets:
Vulture feasts on corpses
You dwell on dead issues
Fully unforgiven of nature, self and others
Downing all forms of constructive strengths.

Inherent in everyman is the ability to feel:
But be not abashed, retrojecting in Ziklag
Get a craic and craze to pursue
Overtake and recover all…

Why sojourn continually amid spilled milk?
Even He who marked the borders of the earth
And conjured the intricate contents of the heart
Supererogated the sorry state of the faithful in the Ark
To achieve a new earth of divine rainbow mark.

Pick up desired colors for your dreams
Get your duende for Tomorrow never knows
What Today is cooking with Yesterday
For a seamless stainless road to Tomorrow

NOTE

The poem opens with an analysis of passage of time- yesterday, today
and tomorrow. It notes the chances of having unfortunate situations
yesterday that tend to hamper today, which if not well handled will
result in an unfortunate tomorrow. It concludes on the need to always
move on, on a positive ground regardless of situation, hoping for a
better tomorrow, rather than dwelling on dead matters.

30
YOU DON'T NEED A TITLE

Do you hope to be relevant in the scheme of things?
Are they asking you what you've brought to the table?
Bothered by your team's emotional intelligence?
All you need do is solve problems:
He who provides solution provides leadership,
He who provides leadership gives direction, earns respect,
He who is respected has leverages from all corners,
He who enjoys leverages performs better, on a continuum
Search and locate solutions to problems, not a title.
As you pay the piper, you'll dictate the tune.
Somehow, but surely.

◄———— NOTE ————►

Simple and direct, the poem posits that we all have capacity to lead, or exert some forms of influence, as a tool to be relevant in life. The mainstay of this is that "he who provides solution provides leadership, he who provides leadership gives direction and earns respect, he who is respected has leverages from all corners, he who enjoys leverages performs better, improving on a continuum..."

31

IN PURSUIT OF THE TENDER PLANT

No nation can be funnier than us
In our ceaseless search for leadership
Where nefarious pot-bellied hags hold sway
With brimming systemic corruptions:
A planned wiley concurrent accidents
Recycling us subitaneous triple-chinned charlatans:
Blinded scrapmen instead of visioners
Crafty men in mold of craftsmen
Disgraceful dissents in lieu of graceful gems
And heartless bosses rather than artless builders
All chop-loge snollygosters with Conley coleworts.

Is there a dearth of visioners
In almost every sphere of endeavors
That the ruthless root out our patrimony
With carnivorous reckless abandonments
And yet no quaesitum for our bedeviled quests?
Perhaps we can procure by ICB
If our failed tissue paper money can afford one
Since we import even toothpicks from abroad
A regrettable rabid regression by enervated leadership
And sorrowfully shameful shame of shameless systems!
We have craned fruitlessly for too long
I think it is time we look Up not around!

Who is on the Tower to show us the Ray
Repairers of the breach with confident hope
The Ray of hope the people truly deserve?

◄——— NOTE ———►

This is a satirical work with focus on the problem of leadership
prevalent in Nigeria- "Blinded scrapmen instead of visioners, Crafty
men in mold of craftsmen, Disgraceful dissents in lieu of graceful
gems, and heartless bosses rather than artless builders. All chop-loge
snollygosters with Conley coleworts." The poet therefore calls out to
know if there are still chances of getting visioners to the different
spheres of the country to pilot her from all knotty issues by being
"Repairers of the breach with confident hope, the Ray of hope the
people truly deserve?"

32
DOWN ON MY KNEELS

Down on my kneels…
Sadly my current posture
All in unwanted location
Of coercive utter surrender
But the Rightful Judge smiles
Said I should alight my high horse
Be contrite to digest the injunction
Oh clay! He says to me
Cease careless struggle
With the Omniscient Potter.

Now full of joy and joyful
This Torch's touch is different
That delivers from cave obscure
Into intended marvelous Light's light

◀——— NOTE ———▶

Technically, when people are on their kneels, especially voluntarily, it shows penitence and trust in God, but if brought down by circumstances of life, it becomes worrisome. This was the state of the poet before he got rejuvenated by the "Omniscient Potter" which brought him so much joy as he ventured into "intended marvelous Light's light."

33
GROWING UP

Growing up
Is Going up
I'm desirous of cheering up
In the quest to move up
And the way I was wired up
I was afraid to screw up
That even if I would wound up
Personally, would want to be fired up
But how do I get jazzed up?
Even as I continued driving up
Lest I give up
Knowing the events would all be summed up
Through a doable but uphill actions' round-up
For that was the dream before I woke up
But you gotta look up
Only God is up!

A funny piece and tone with a serious message. It's a monorhyme on
the word 'up'

34

THE FEVER FROM FLIVVER

Again, I sigh like one awaiting fate of a split decision
It is not of coercion or the force of estoppel
But the dawning reality of a demeaning decrepit car
Under the weight of wrong and misplaced priorities…
And previewing the impending needless journey
The more I see me in mediaeval armaments
Secured in the insecurity of veracious visible realism
With no chance lever for a clever corps cum core criminal
And forthwith, the music commenced for all to dance.

As the arrhythmic sound of the costumed car
Blended with the rhythm of our angry agonies
But no one queried why this car or why this route…
With our disjointed joints assembled in a heap
Cladded with clothes whose color changes with the climate
Under the dictates of the endless windy and dusty road
And the grubbiness of overlapping
"Sweet sweats of the inmates"
We arrived.

We arrived to see the meds we longed to see
For restorative reliefs desiring the pleasure
Of our reported awful experiences
Then we know we are stuck
For another four-year term in Hades

How we wished we ate and still have our cakes
Voting right despite devouring the stolen spoils?
Our rights, now a franchised merchandise.

<hr>

◄──── NOTE ────►

A satirical work that employs an impending journey in an old car,
coupled with other unfavourable conditions, to drive home a political
message, which was not revealed until the denouement at the end of
the poem. It shows the corrupt election process which results in almost
same discomfort's for both the leaders and the masses. The poet
regretted not taking the corrupt politicians' money whilst still voting
right, consequently- "our rights, now a franchised merchandise."

35

AFRICA

For how long shall you remain blindfelled?
For how long shall you heed the western dictates
To seize from being the tools in its workshop
The state that has brought you nothing
But abundant blitz in bliss' stead?

Africa please remember
Remember the blaze of those years
Years that your men of acumen
Voyaged painfully disarmed under duress.
And some lugubriously jettisoned with indifference.

Oh! I cannot fathom.
The essence of these tumult by turns
That shamefully describes your existence
When you ought to unite units
To fight your common adversary

Africa I say you have to remember
That the West prospers in your distress
Gathering fortunes from frequent fracas
You designed for its merriment
At the expense of your black glory

Africa do you have to be reminded
The four-century of colonialism
And the reigning neo-colonialism
That makes it the horse before your cart?

Africa strive to remember
That liberation is never late
Just tell your empty heads to be caudal not
But get optical help for their cecutiency
To see beyond their noses and halt groping
Failure to decide is a decision.

◄———— NOTE ————►

Inspired by David Diop's 'Africa my Africa,' the poet rhetorically
addressed a personified Africa on the need for true emancipation from
the West. He reminds Africa of the precolonial troubles and the fact
that only Africans can genuinely solve African problem. He therefore
concludes with a recommendation of quality visionary leadership to
achieve the intended goal.

36

SACRILEGE

Oh sacrilegious arbiter!
Where is the fountain of thy arbitration
That you mete and dole power arbitrary
Inventing a cistern for despotic derailed reign
When empirically you are profane to civil rule
Leaving your nature for hype-up duties
Like a bull in a China's shop
To bumbazedly bulldoze the rule of law
Though you lack the law to rule
Can't you take a look round the globe
To see the Roman civic crown
Saying no to the Roman cit
Unlike your firm grip to Abuja seat
Professing transitions to nowhere
Taking advantage of our fear to die to live?

◀──── NOTE ────▶

The poem is set in a military rule, a situation the poet greatly decries, as
he describes military as "profane to civil rule" and consequently
incapable of upholding the rule of law because it "...lack the law to
rule". He enjoined the military to stay at their bases just like those of
developed nations, instead of venturing into politics and deceiving the
masses with programmes of "...transitions to nowhere."

37
CELEBRATED IMPUNITY

Listen people of sacred lands
Where democracy reigns
They have dismanned the symbol
Of our democratic mandate
And an unprecedented unity in diversities
A sure by-product of
Their arbitrary clique's tutelage
In the same submarine that conveyed
Dele Giwa and Rewani and Kudi and Gani
After Adesanya and Enahoro among others
Missed the tyrant's death-train by the whisker.
A sure trip of no return

All saw them brandished
The infamous invisible Abuja tea-sword
Yet by deceit, urged us
To behold their clean white hands with which they
Bullishly buried the manifestoed Hope-1993
Our democratic sweat of June the great
Perhaps the freest fairest history possesses
Without facing the music of their fair crude cruelty
Not even Kofi's boss faulted them
A group we know not the stand it stands:

An audience or actor?
Let's just say beast of no-nation.

But that is not enough excuse
For the greatest black nation
To have her glory cowedly hospitalized
Without diagnosis or medication
But rather brutalization that draws her
Into a dance with rites she shouldn't know
What next?

|◄──── NOTE ────►|

This is set in Nigeria, around the botched transition programme of
Gen. Ibrahim Babangida, which led to the incarceration of the
universally acclaimed winner, Chief MKO Abiola and his eventual
death in custody. The poet decries the role played by the government
and international organizations, especially United Nations team, led by
the then General Secretary, Kofi Anan. He alleged that they tried to do
same to other political elites but failed. He concluded by hinting at the
consequences, but also seized the chance to charge everyone to work
together for the betterment of the nation, despite the rot at the top.

38

NIGERIA! A QUIVER FULL OF ARROWS

"Nigeria, my beloved country
Working together is the key
Nigeria my beloved country Her future is You and Me.
I know a lot about my country
I know a lot because I care
I know a lot about Nigeria
I know a lot because I care"

Yes, I know a lot about Nigeria
A nation prophetically ordained and formed
A nation divinely endowed and established
A land divided by waters and diverse tongues
A land located beyond the rivers of Ethiopia
A nation of merchants and itineraries
Whose ambassadors cover the whole earth.
I know a lot about you, great nation of great people
I know a lot because I care.
Probe yourself now, you that awaits the New Nigeria
How much of the Old do you know?
How much of this land do you care to know?
I am a youth is not an excuse, for I am one also.

You might be a child of history but
You are the parent of the future

I am not in position of authority is not tenable
You don't need a title to lead
God designed all to have a domain of influence
How far have you been helping in building the nation?
It is too expensive to wipe out the ancient landmarks
Nigeria in retrospect is a must-know for you and me.

Nigerians, before we are so called
Were greatly resilient, though seemingly backward,
We're courageous…
We had "…proud warriors in the ancestral savannah"
That endured the four-century of indifferent slave trade.
That had our men of acumen jettisoned lugubriously.
The Aba women riot of 1929
The esteemed checks and balances of the Oyo mesi
The entrenched nationalist movements of ancient Egbas
And the assertive zeal of the northern Jihadist
All attest to the claim of our nobility and black pride.
Nigeria, is a quiver full of arrows, arrows of diverse species
Today, my song is on the specie of leadership!

The beautiful beast of colonialism came sojourning
Disguised as international trade and cultural exchanges
It ravaged and drained our pure serenity and endowment
Though it brought faith and modern education in its wake
It was a double-edged sword of guided civilization
A monster we fought tooth and nail to assuage
Herbert Macaulay, Zik of Africa, Obafemi Awolowo
And other learned progressives within and without Nigeria
Championed the Nationalist movements to mount pressure
For self-governance with total emancipation in focus.

In 1953, Anthony Enahoro moved the evergreen motion
For independence by the year 1956, but was not applauded
By the British inspired and tutelage northerners
That replaced this classical motion of history with another
"As soon as possible" was the pessimists' phrase.

Although God alone knows best
I can conclude by critical inferences from empirical surveys
That certain time-bomb statements migrated
From London to Kano-
"These southerners are learned, exposed and equipped
To dominate economic power,
So, hold on to political power tenaciously
If need be, by military might
Lest you become slaves in your own land"
And so, the seed of discord was planted
Right from the foundation.
Among hitherto collaborative protectorates and brothers,
Thus, tearing apart our healthy fraternity
Paving way for distrust, fear, greed,
Among other devilish devices
To be the unfortunate tools of programmed governance
When the coloured colonialism came on 1st October, 1960
Entrusting power via systemic orchestrations
In the least qualified Teacher Tafawa Balewa
A surety of divide and rule for Britain's gain
Neo-colonialism is the name of the fraudulent game.

We tried; we tried in 1963 to cut-off this unbiblical cord
But we could only get a Republic
A Republic of insatiable warring kingdoms

A year of census, inter- and intra-party's cacophonies
A season of political detentions, killings
And State of Emergency
Or you think it's a new concept?
It was indeed the season of national monumental losses
Humanly, materially and otherwise
We have been killing Nigeria for long.

In rare celerity my friends! On January 15th, 1966
Major Chukwuma Kaduna Nzeogwu
A lecturer in the Nigerian Defense Academy
Led a group of young Army Officers
To sack the Federal and Regional Governments
Leading to revolts and deaths, and more deaths,
All around the western region…
How much of the old do you know?

On January 16th, the following day,
The man that ruled Nigeria for just a day,
The pioneering Interim President if you care to know…
It is not a new concept too! I guess many aren't aware,
Dr. Nwafor Orizu, heralded on National Radio
That our chicken-hearted, gun-threatened
And centrifugal Council of Ministers
Has unanimously invited the Military to administer Nigeria
It sounds quizzical to you too?
The entire world is, but a theater and our nation,
Nigeria is the very drama stage of actions. Expect more!

So, by INVITATION,
The military had its baptism of fire in our politicking:

The General Officer Commanding the Nigerian Army
Major General Johnson Thomas Umunakwe Aguiyi-Ironsi
Accepted the invitation
And thus congratulated us for such a privilege?
"The Military Government of the
Federal Republic of Nigeria has taken over
The interim administration of Nigeria
Following the invitation of the Council of Ministers
The invitation has been accepted
I have been formally invested with authority
As head of the National Government
And Supreme Commander of the Nigerian Armed Forces."

He spent his reign trying
And trying to do what he was not trained for
He ended up as a showman carrying
And ruling with the power of crocodile
He was profane to civil rule
And the hype-up duty jettisoned his wit
Till the revengeful coup d'état
Engineered by the Military Mighty Might of the North
Imposed on us, the youthful and energetic Gowon
As our 3rd President.

General Yakubu Gowon came onboard gallantly
Pledged Reconstruction, Rehabilitation and Reconciliation
But the civil war during which he merrily married
Overwhelmed his desired and projected
Going On With One Nigeria:
As "funeral piles ate up the forest" from frequent fracas
Colossal clashes of cruel claims

And counter catastrophic claims while
The emissaries of rift ran helter-skelter, groping abroad.

We were all casualties
Of the made in Nigeria cancerous wicked war
Though kudos for the infrastructural additions to our lives
Gowon perpetuated
The demise of the Nigerian flag's famous green
As the oil boom displaced our agricultural prowess
A problem we have been battling till today,
Even with a farmer as president-
And Nigeria became a frustrating mono-economy.

Someone felt he could do better,
In the corrupted office of Nigeria's presidency
As another coup brought-in Murtala Mohammed
As the 4th President
A seeming saviour, laudable, plausible
But in just six months friends,
Got swallowed in the botched coup of Dimpka & Co. Plc.

Then Obasanjo stepped in by share grace but gallantly
Promising, among other things,
A continuation of the programme of peace
And handing over of power
To the people's popular mandate
But his 'International Thief Thief' calculated projects
His padi padi and rigimo government
And the Operation Feed the Nation's food for all
Targeted at restoring Nigeria's Agricultural Prowess
Filled his cupboard with demonic legion of skeletons.

On October 1, 1978, he laid the foundation,
Sets the record of the 1st President to touch petrol price
As the National Farm metamorphosed to Obasanjo Farms.
Spiritually, Obasanjo erected high places for Baal
Importing gods from far and near
To complement the works of the local gods
To de-fertilize and debase the nation totally,
It was tagged Festac '77
Ebora owu brought his family's familiar spirits
To a sumptuous communion
And to cover up his secret, shady
But humble national thefts
He facilitated FEDECO to rig the election of 1979
In favour of Alhaji Sheu Shagari
As Awo's UPN, favoured to win the election,
Vowed to probe his past, present and future.

I am sure Obasanjo must have regretted
His humble federal thefts
When he saw, the large-scale loot
Meted our treasury by his successors-
Shagari wobbled and fumbled indefatigably and relentlessly
The economy suffered more than never before
In a bewildering rapidity, in the hands of these stealers
But he perpetuated himself to plunder a second term
With Austerity Measure for the masses
But pomp for the Political Elites
And it became a shame to be called a Nigerian.

I do not know whether to say the 6.5 and 7th
Or the 7th Presidents

But it took the monstrous leadership heads
Popularly called the Buhari/Idiagbon regime
To decapitate the bulls' brains
And Nigerians rejoiced
To see their familiar friendly foe again
The Military in Politics.
It was the season for observance
Of true Austerity Measures as
Imprisoned food items were liberated and auctioned
The naira got new colours to add to the woes of hoarders
And he exposed the path to the corrupt-wealth
Of drug merchants in high places
But when the frowned face and ethical standards
Of this rugged plant choked lawless men and women
In low and high places, as his military regimented
Commands could not be easily understood or obeyed
Intrigues and strategies of deliverance
From Idiagbon went-on quickly under-ground
To combat him, his MAMSER, NDLEA, his
War Against Indiscipline and other
Perceived poisonous products of his government
Notwithstanding the ensuing sanity,
Discipline and probity in public offices.

So suddenly, they struck! Yes! He struck
Beheading the monstrous heads-of-state
After the cabal within and without
Lured Idiagbon from an unholy to a holy ground
The eternally ambiguous smiles of Babangida emerged
To the loving applause of the liberated lawless Nigerians.

Join me to welcome the programmes of our
No. 8 President, Mr. Cool Face, IBB:
He tried Structural Adjustment Programme, SAP
He tried Second-tier Foreign Exchange Market, SFEM
Foreign Currency Domiciliary Account
And Bureau De Change
National Economic Reconstruction Fund, NERFUND
Introduced the National Electoral Commission, NEC,
Humphrey Nwosu's child
Debt Rescheduling and Debt Conversion devices,
At least without traveling
Dir. of Food, Road and Rural Infrastructure, DFRRI
Nigerian Agricultural Cooperative Bank, NACB
Nigerian Agric. Cooperative Marketing Org., NACMO
And the Peoples Bank, among other mega failures
Only for the evil genius to conclude
With neither remorse nor shame
That Nigeria's peculiar nature
Transcends all economic postulations…
He shut Tertiary Institutions
With disdain for over 8 months in 1993 alone
Proscribed challenging dailies and sent many to toil
In unavailable labour markets
Placed embargo on employment
To better the lots of millions of NYSC graduates
Doctors strike with the speed of light,
Leaving hospital inmates dead or dying

The evil genius botched many alleged coups
And sent defenseless alleged participants
On journeys of no return

While he lived secured in the hurriedly funded
Rocky New National Capital, an unprecedented
Devilish achievement in human history
He quashed many transitions programmes
Including our best general election in history
Leading many to unmerited graves
Within and without the scenes of revolts
And the slap of God beclouded him
For the blood of the innocents
Oh! The gut of our International Bad Boy failed him,
In the wake of the pressure that followed
Perhaps for MKO's weight
Interjected life and destiny or the people's mandate.
He danced to the beat of several
Violent peaceful protesting drums of June 12
To release another ever-green clause in Nigeria's politics
"...I therefore STEP ASIDE"
The evil genius, devil's incarnate and born-again democrat
Stepped aside audaciously into a stolen 50-bedroom edifice
While the unsuspecting, ambitiously blind-felled
Chief Earnest Shonekan stepped-in
As the Interim President for the second time in history,
Remember 1966?
What a dramatic and ambitious move
Like those of timeouts in basketball game
As the hitherto successful capitalist,
Manager and Industrialist tossed to and fro in office
Before the programmed umpire sent him packing
Sacking the sacrificial lamb
Offered to calm the Yorubas and the south
With Oladipupo Diya

As another credible lamb of peace offering, deputising.

Whether this umpire did better or not, thou knowest…
All I know is that he acted the Locust
That ate what the Palmerworm left
Nigeria's movement became hydra-headed, o ma se o!
Pressure groups and the pens
Were sardined and geishad with indifference
The only sword in Israel was with the king,
And was mightier than legions of pen
As he perpetuated countless wrong deeds with confidence
Not only did he lack the law to rule,
He killed the rule of law
To dehumanize and desensitize the privileged remnants.

All that needed to be wrong went wrong unabatedly
Till he was declared the only one
Capable of governing Nigeria
He got the nod to just change his camouflage
With agbada on a platter of fraud
Nobody could handle the threading weights
Of this monstrous elephant.
As respected musicians and celebrities
Swallowed shame and sanity to praise the cat
That fed fat on the national meat
Together with his clan, stocking lots abroad
As Abacha's foreign reserves
Competes favourably with Nigeria's
It was a comprehensive
Desensitization of the national psyche.

But hurray for thunder! An act of divine mercy
For indeed, we were all helpless and changing camps
He slept permanently, allegedly
Between two divinely assigned imported angels
And got a befitting burial
After a secret mobile lying-in-state
Behind a cargo plane.
Then, our indefatigable schemers went to work,
In the demonized self-centred studio
Of the cabal-militants to release another album
From the military archival materials
General Abdul-salami Abubakar unanimously emerged
Ahead of the Lagos proven, hurriedly elevated Barao…
Buba Marwa, Albarka Air that aired Lagos' wealth
As the 11th President of the Federal Republic of Nigeria.

General Abdul-Salami Abubakar!
Was he another child of necessity?
He was the cankerworm
That perfected the locust's appetite
Possessor of the subtle special sensational guile,
The meshai that prepared the tea of life for MKO
Abiola died in a war he had no business fighting
The only way forward to peace from the June 12 agitators
As contained in the master-script
Of the omniscient writer, director and narrator
Well bounded and transported
From the 50-bedroom hell of the real executioner
For immediate acting
On the world's forever famous drama stage, Nigeria.

Abubakar discovered the loots
Shared the loot, looted the loot and looted afresh
Just buying time for what the evil genius was cooking
And when it did, it necessitated a release and a journey
A release of Obasanjo from jail and a journey to Ota
To encourage another sacrificial lamb
To appease the Yorubas and the land
And when the dog was exhorted
And ready to return to his vomit
The only military acceptable to the civilians
The only southerner acceptable to the northerners
The only ogboni Christian acceptable to the Muslims
Was registered, funded and rigged into power
As our 12th President.

"He came out of prison to be king
Although he was born poor in his kingdom"
He came-in foolhardy as ever
He came-in in the wake of serious prophetic alerts
He came-in to execute the devil's agenda
And to set the unbeatable records of evil consequences
"Better a poor and wise youth, my friend
Than an old and foolish king
Who will be admonished no more"
It was the second coming of the gallant gorilla
Brother Matthew Okikiola Aremu Olusegun Obasanjo
Against all odds and hypocritical obedience
To prophetic alerts by this King Agag
Then he promised to appoint prophets
If need be, for the interest of the nation

And the saying pleased the priests, Pharisees
And Sadducees of our land.
This spared detainee King Agag, famous farmer,
Became the caterpillar perfecting the inglorious jobs
Of the Palmerworm, the Locust and the Cankerworm
He promised to fight corruption to a standstill
That yielded a timely fruit:
Nigeria jumped to the disgracing position
Of second most corrupt nation worldwide
Family Life, the basic unit of any society,
Broke to disgracing shambles nationwide
With strong shameful evidence even in the 1st family
Occultism got to its climax
In the time of this man of evil fraternities
As blood flowed freely at the Obafemi Awolowo University
When the Black Axe Confraternity
Took charge on July 10, 1999 with all implicated
And confirmed cultists freed on toothless bails
By the Abuja-tutored Chief Magistrate's Court.
Still thirsty for more bloods for heaven knows why
He ordered for Odi to be massacred,
A 15,000 peopled community leveled to ground zero
With no trace of earlier habitation and women
At nearby Choba callously raped without recompense.

Poverty Alleviation Programme
Ended-up aggravating poverty
Incessant tourist movements built us no good fortune
Chike Obi must have been ashamed to be a citizen
Of a country that jubilated over a dubious debt-relief
After spending fortune with wicked-silently covered terms

I remember he told the well-used Audu Ogbe in 2004
That "'Nigeria is moving to the cruising level
At a cruising speed..."
And truly we rapidly relegated at the speed of light
Little did we realize that our brand of demon-crazy
Is specially designed to kill democrats.

Transferred aggressions and vengeance
Seemed the fool's appetite- "That thing wey
I no chop well in the 70s, don come my way,"
He seems to say, as events unfolds,
Revealing the animal called man.
Totally defiant to words of logic, sanity or civilisation
As he recompenses and re-christened
His chattered spiritual fathers, idiots!
In his piggy embarrassing looks
Of un-cultured concocted triple chin
And his foolish pride deteriorated
In his dubiously forged second coming
With a special resolve not to listen
To his ill-fated Special Advisers.

His first point of call was petrol price, hiked!
Executed five times in ten months,
An average of every two-month increase
At a choice-time to add credence and clarity to
His cruel message of power without compassion.

The increase in June 2003 was just after he was sworn-in,
A swift dividend of democracy?

The increase in October 2003 was on Independence Day
To foster our dependent independence
The increase in December 2003 was during Christmas
A Yuletide blessing from a Christian ebora
The first increase in May 2004
Was when he asked us to pray and fast for 3 days
And when the praying and fasting
Were accepted by his doomed political gods
We got the blessing of another increase
From this callous civil criminal On 29th May, 2004
For us to celebrate Demon-crazy Day
From June 1, 2000, how many petrol price regimes?
You can try your wit on the figure;
My own focus is the impact!
God! Do not use hurricane Ivan or Katrina
To deliver us from this vain oil dependency
They've used our wealth to snatch our health
And strength to their own delight

Questions:
Have you ever wondered the make-up
Of this animal called man?
Aren't you tired of these sufferings and sadistic games?
Shall the leaders of tomorrow watch them
Destroy the tomorrow, our tomorrow, today?
An American president resigned
For document-evidence got from the opposition illegally
He stole no dollar, he gave no jeep to his girlfriend,
He bought no privatized company like Atiku…
A Japanese president resigned because of only allegations

Our leaders shielded our *Executhieves* from the Law…
They called it PDP Family Affair.

Then came a time that the house was divided against itself,
God is good, all the time. All the time, God is good!
In its wake was the doom of the third term agenda
And former allies washed their dirty *bantes* outside
It was like a typical nagging home of an African polygamist
Yet they sat tight, shamelessly hoping for good cover-ups:
They disseminated bad seeds
And then sought and prayed for crop failure
Truly, all whose gains are from the ruins of this land
Shall not stand sure, Amen!
23 governors were investigated, out of 30
15 with enough evidence to start court proceedings
And a plan to recall past leaders to face the wrath of law
Despite the list being a mincemeat,
A mere representation I can say, as Ribadu was
Divinely given cheap evidence from heavenly places
…But he lived up to his assessed disposition,
No justice done.

Aha! Let's just assume Nigeria is a man,
Single and seriously searching
Sister can you marry him, risk your future?
Or if a lady, your lovely, wedded bride brother
To stake your strength and destiny?
Did you say God forbid?
That is the old foolhardy hag they turned Nigeria to:
Despised, unsought, undreamed by any nation,
Even beggarly ones!

Yet the tapeworms were not done with us yet…
But we have GOD O!
Our God that confused all the Baalams
At the deluding CONFAB
Even when they mapped out schemes
Of indirect perpetuation to cover their backs
But an Arrow of God shattered their dreams!
It rained and it failed! Just as heaven wanted it
Self-succession turned Self-destruction
IBB killed Babangida, OBJ killed Obasanjo…
Atiku ti ku! Gone to Gongola
The blood of Bola Ige,
Who failed to turn stones to bread
And Abiola that paid the supreme sacrifice
For democracy hunted them.

Ours is a country where a serving prisoner
Mysteriously, won an election from jail
Where a performing governor was sent away from office
For disobeying his political god-father…
One was even abducted despite being the CSO of his state
As cheap deposition of royalties by pimp governors ensued
Just as a sitting president mobilized money
For personal gains on the guise of a National Library
Whose archives is likened to a family bookshelf
Is there anything impossible for our government to do?
Tell them, there is nothing impossible for God to do too
This is God's own country.

He likes to be praised, taking preeminence

Even in the face of imminent expiration of his term
As the third term agenda ended in a kaput
Tracks, acts and tracts needed coverage
Beyond even forensic audit trails
So, Obasanjo's devilish ingenuity came to fore
"I'll get them a successor
That would make them long for me"
The inherent demons uttered voices
From his innermost being as he went to the house of
Sheu Musa Y'Adua, his former vice president where
He wrestled and brought a younger Umaru Musa Y'Adua
Out of the grip of death as the 13th President of Nigeria
To silence Buhari and Atiku's presidential hopes.

Like a diamond from the mud
Umaru Y'Adua brought a rare ray of hope
Acknowledging becoming president
On the wings of a flawed process
He promised and started uniting units
He chose Ebele Jonathan to be his Vice President
Siting his naivety in terms of wholesale corruption
And with a seven-point agenda of Infrastructure,
Power and Energy, Food security, Wealth creation,
Transport, Land reforms, Security and Education
He sets sail summoning serious courage.
The spirit proposes but his body could not dispose
Just as contained in the devilish script of OBJ the impostor
Medical Tourism was the bane of the seeming rare gem
He, notwithstanding quelled
The aggression of the South through amnesty

Introduced promising Electoral Reforms
And improved international relations
But had to part ways with his vision
For a child of necessity to be born
As a voice from heaven sounded, "he's no longer with us"
A Doctrine of Necessity transferred power to GEJ
Bending to the peoples' heavy united voice
Compelling voices like those that stepped IBB aside
After a prolonged battle of cabals' coverups
Of a shameful senseless fraudulent power vacuum
To deliver us from unprovoked secrets plots
Of a budding military takeover.

So Ebele Goodluck Jonathan
Came as 14th on May 5, 2010
The first from the south-south to clinch the seat
Rising to take his boss' position
For the second time in quick succession
But this second was a big claw
In the wheel of PDP's rotational presidency
And the schemers were quick to point it out
One even loudly promised unequivocally
To make the country ungovernable
But Jonathan moved swiftly on the wings of Sapele water
Running around for like-minds kitikiti
Like a shoeless man on a hot paved-way
To let them know he can sink the ship if further despised
And the intransigence quiet storm was calmed for a season.
Armed only with a testimony
Of being born without any shoe
Just like the zoo inmates he loved and trained to care for

He forged plans to manage this bigger homo sapiens' zoo.

He tried on promoting observance of the Rule of Law
Rebased GDP for the first time in over a decade
As Nigeria became the largest economy in Africa
Overtaking South Africa and Egypt
He enacted the Freedom of Information Act
And we started to have our voices honoured
Continued Y'Adua's electoral reforms, all geared towards
Non-interference in electoral outcomes and
Promotion of peace… and Peace
The Peace was extravagant, loquacious and entertaining
A handy comic-relief from eco-political hardships
The peace was then confronted by Boko Haram et all
And a time-bomb of infightings of the PDP family
Bringing the promises to fulfilment was clearly inevitable:
They made the country ungovernable and he sank the ship.
School girls were abducted in broad day light on a platter.
Just as Y'Adua observed, he had little acumen in stealing
But he wisely employed thieves to help him harness what
He can get in addition to his guaranteed hourly ekpeteshi
Sequel to which Diezani helped shipped loots to Otueke
After getting more than enough for herself and household
He instituted an expensive but applauded and respected
National Conference in 2014
But could not succeed himself in office
To execute the recommendations
He can never forget the people's oil subsidy revolt of Ojota
Helpless and humbled by a national quest for change
He listened to the voice of reasoning
To ensure the first inter-party

And peaceful civilian to civilian transition
A unique defeat of an incumbent in our brand of election
GEJA succumbs to JEGA
To the shame of Orubebe and Fadile

And from the brink, another converted democrat emerged
Mohammadu Buhari came as the 15th President of Naija
And a cow hustler took over from a zoo keeper
In the animal kingdom called Nigeria
He came with lots of perceived prospects
Of an incorruptible character, ably assisted by a pastor
And Professor of Law, a tested Attorney General
It looks like a new horizon for the nation, as he declared:
"I belong to everybody and I belong to nobody"
It was however a rough start marked by mixed progress
As oil revenue dwindled to plunge the nation into recession
Earlier mitigated northern terrorism resurfaced fortified
Insurgency arose in the south by secessionists calls
And the war on corruption was lopsidedly selective
Even the corruption he fought fought him back
Relentlessly, confidently.
Then we realized the body suffered
Because it wasn't well with the head
As he spent a good portion of his tenure abroad
On medical open-secret tourisms
And the nation feared a repeat of Y'Adua's debacle
Some even said the president passed in the process and
Suspicions and allegations of a body-double came to fore
But he came back from the dead
Stronger to win a reelection
Whether as 'say Baba!' or 'say Jubril' no one cares,

Nigeria has been a joke for long,
No joke can hurt us anymore
From then on, it was a cruise into the abyss
Of inconceivable monumental decay
I wished he implemented a tenth
Of the Jonathan's 2014 Conference recommendations
He would have given himself an enduring legacy,
But he seemed an irredeemable forlorn fellow.
Became dictatorial quieting even the youths
In a deadly Bourdillon aided tollgate massacre
Tried to teleguide the next election all to no avail
Got angry and vowed to make it difficult for the deviants
Including changing the colour of the naira
To frustrate their war chest
And the city cried buying naira with naira
To the credit of God-suppose-win Emefiole
The people resolved to exercise their power at the poll
With mobilization for PVC and the Obidient movement
Enough is enough was the chorus on the street
Even the rich also cried but one was the loudest
In the wilderness of uncertainties
Shouting *emi lokan*, it's my turn,
Even in the wake of a failing health
And barrages of known and unknown cupboards
Filled with living skeletons.
Then we were reminded
There were no longer statesmen around
But selfish men whose focus is the next election,
Not the next generation.
Following the practiced path of political brazen harlotry

The kingmakers saw no better person
Than the expired one, drowned in sense of entitlement
Internationally acclaimed fraudster and certificate forger
And indelible footprints of executive thieving
And financial aggrandizement,
With INEC magic
And misguided strengths of disoriented youths
In a systemic corrupt process
Selected ABAT for us as the 16th president.

It was a season of Technical Glitch
Above legislated procedure that halted
The promised direct electronic
Election result transmission
Even the court granted INEC the grace of discretion
Against the dictates of documented procedure
In a lopsided election tribunal
A shameless disruption of the rule of law
For democracy says power flows from the people
But power of Tinubu's stolen election flows from
A Mahmood Yakub inspired glitch
As an excellent and world-honoured BVAS and IReV
Bowed to the weight of our customised corruption
And it is no longer at ease with us.

He started with a policy summersault
An ill-informed and dubious subsidy removal
Targeted immediate and past enemies
To make them face selective vindictive judgments
That shoot-up general price level when introduced
But the high price remained when restored

And the city rejoices as the poor struggle to breathe
Repackaged the customary ethnic dichotomy
In political appointments of colourful mess
And overrated himself in playing big brother of ECOWAS
Empty threats and leaky plans of unwarranted invasions
With everything backfiring on us like nonentities
Naira drowned competing for value with sea shells
It's a season of abductions, among other insecurities again
VAT and other taxes suddenly developed wings
Whilst the traditional budget padding tore
The National Assembly apart
While they sought honour among thieves
Even Ningi the whistle blower swallowed his vomit.
When they opened the book of fate for him
Traditional rulers are being murdered left right and centre
17 soldiers massacred, a sequel to the Coat of Arm
Being surrendered to terrorist king to malign soldiers
Even those at the mercy of the government
Were killed in IDP camps
Expatriate employment levy was introduced
To boost direct foreign investment
Presidential Private jet being used
By the first son to attend parties
And for any dissenting voice against ABAT,
The Lord of the Ring of Thieves
Gbajabiamila threatened three years imprisonment…
Every absurdity has been normalized,
As familitocracy holds sway
First son and first lady coming ahead
Of constituted order of protocol
We now seem to have the

Office of the 1st Son
Office of the 1st Lady
Office of the 1st In-law
Office of the 1st Friend
Office of the 1st Housemaids…

If you can just explore the womb of time
Nigeria's tragedies are easily foretold
It is a self-fulfilling prophecy
Telling the truth totally truly victimizes,
Better deodorize their conks to be saved
Student union no longer a conscious layer but
Now incorporated into the cruelty at the top
Due to the inspired bureaucratic sabotage
Since there is no justice if murdered fighting for truth
Our pangs of birth brought us no joy
Because a monster's born to be bred
The marriage of our
Thesis and Antithesis resulted in no Synthesis.
Our current trajectory is not sustainable my people
We're right now in a peculiar state of nature
Kangun kangun kangun a kangun sibikan.

They've been used to thresh us, to prune us and prepare us
They always come with a pledge of a change for better
But all we constantly have is an identical difference
Children of Issachar, it is time for the new wine
A seeming guile has taken over our nation
Rise to welcome the dawn of a new era
Rise to welcome the spirit of, and the New Nigeria!

It is time for Nigeria to fulfill her prophetic destiny!
The four winds of the earth now on a coalition course
Where are the Joseph's companies?
When will the revolution begin, with you?
How will the seemingly godly-poor
Swap position with the corrupt-rich?
When shall we stop groping around these temporary joys?
When shall we wipe out the devilish traditional rulers,
And reduce the khaki and khaki-agbadas
To the state of errand boys,
Drunken men that brought the east wind upon us
To put an end to these step dances
And deft political moves?!
How do you think the economy of this nation will recover?
I mean faster than that of Japan?
Not in the hands of these highly recycled foolhardy pilots
It is a function of the fulfillment of individual destinies!
Has God shown you the great destiny He has for you?
Do you want to rise above your circumstances?
Then get your scepter back, the Lord has need of it!
Elevate your expectation and demand for your own field
Put on your shoes for it is time to thread upon serpents
The blessings of the son must not elude you!
For the tender plant to grow, the rugged must go
Can anyone finish discussing the case of Nigeria?

◄━━━ NOTE ━━━►

This is a wake-up call to all Nigerians in particular and Africans in general. With literary allusions to JP Clark's "Casulities" and other works, the poet heralded the leadership crisis in Nigeria right before colonialism till independence was obtained. The struggles and intrigues of the Nigerian brand of politics were pictorialy presented in a somewhat humourous but intellectual and well research plot. For simplicity sake, he enumerated the pros and cons of each and every leader of the country from inception till date and the response of the people at every point in time. It is a good read for anyone that wants to know the true history of Nigeria in a less tragic format.

39

THE PLEDGE

I pledge to Niger Area my area
To be observant and conversant
Lamenting and commenting
On the unpatriotic intrigues and strategies
Of her dedicated fraud merchants in leadership
That excellently abrade her endowed wealth
Introducing it to their family menu
In a manner that suggests invaluable calorie
In their newfound diet
Which they devour with great appetite
At the expense of the dying owners
With special disdain for the oblivious gutter blood
Rendered harmless by their forlorn status
And living in unmerited sadomasochism
As their uniformed MPs collude with safari men
As well as some fooled pessimist
Are intoxicated at the great expense
Abstaining from the dreaded democracy
A mountainous menace to their illicit joy
And daring the barking of the watchdogs
They carved colored goodwill among their allies
A surety for the fountain of their joy
And forgetting that He that sharpened hearts edges
Always maintain perfect surveillance
To faithfully reward as He deem fit.

As for me and my liefs
We shall busily endure and pray
For them to face their music
And for the masses' Jericho wall
To fall beneath their feet
So help me God.

NOTE

This tries to mimic the Nigerian National Pledge satirically, alluding the
endemic bad leadership, especially their utter disdain for the interest of
the masses in relation to their selfish appetites. He concludes by
prayerfully showing the readers his solidarity for the attainment of a
New Nigeria, together his family and like-minds.

40
AT DEATH

A permanent pause are labourers' toils
The warring days unwillingly over
On the bank distant far
Rested the ship cold
There to be comforted
Where many are taken
To the truthful Judge
Who weighs lives and times
There where the sinners
Look upon the cross
To know all Christ's love
At His feet in paradise

There where Satan's might
Their salt cannot murder
For Christ shielded
And died for their souls

Soil for soil thus
Our language turns
Spread for our rest
Till that last day

◄———— NOTE ————►

This is a reflective poem on the significant impact of death, how sudden it can be and the consequent feeling of the bereaved. It also hints on life after death, talking about subsequent judgement of the dead by God, "Where many are taken to the truthful Judge who weighs lives and times..." In conclusion, he gave insight into how the dead are honoured at the burial site before being committed to mother earth.

41

ODE TO MKO

What is this life to us?
A mere cloud it seems.
A moving clay in the mourning
Is lifeless at night timing.

What is our breath like?
With a strolling shadow it seems alike
That now boldly appear like a new son
But dwindles with the drowning sunset's sun

Your shadow in July faded
Faded with the repented sun
Ha! You are no more found
Gone totally from us with no fun

Liberty you have from pains
Of these worldly strains
Free to rest in the Lord
Where the nicest of sleeps abound

But the shield of God I crave
For your legacy, with you now in the grave
Even to your place distant above
Till we meet with works to prove

Adieu my distant lief
Sad to see your life cut in brief
May your soul rest from mourning
Like the river's taste in the morning

Delighted I am for your happier hope
In lieu of the cruelly abducted 1993's hope
For though your body's soiled
Your soul with the Lord refreshed

NOTE

This was written in honour of Late MKO, Abiola, the acclaimed winner
of June 12, 1993 Presidential Election, who was incarcerated sequel to
his self-declaration after the election was brutally quashed by the
government of Gen. Ibrahim Babangida. It is filled with praises for
him and prayers for the sustenance of his legacies, whilst hoping his
soul find rest in the Lord.

42

AJUWAYAH

Like an assuming plaintiff
I waited to face the music
Of my final examination
Which came belatedly without ills
Setting state almost at once
For the mandatory National Service
The call-up of which refused to come
And when it did lacked identity
Then I resolved is without Nigeria
But someone mysteriously fixed the place
At the far east of the country
Calling it a newborn baby
Then I envisaged troubles
Of a pioneering service-squad
Without travelling acumen.

Notwithstanding, I set for mission
Saying my prayers solemnly
With the sound of Ekene Dili.
The ways deeply endless
I felt like saying no
To slavery or what it is?
But common company goals
Filled my tank and tidy the filter
To continue the lonesome episode.

The first pause we had
Was a café called half
Of what the journey would be
All things being equal.
Progressing then was tedious
Just as returning impracticable.
The city hostile hot, volatile
And kindly charging high prices
Through zealous exploiters.
I ate what I saw but not need
And my needs exceeded my wants
Paid for meat I couldn't defeat
Which was apprehended by hungrier passers-by
That grabbed it more out of right than appeal
So I took solace in paracetamol
The only familiar thing for my belly
At such an hour plagued bewilderment.

The adventure continued now absent-minded
Surrendering indifferently to
The travails of the endless journey.
I lost my eyes I'd have slumber
I lost my mind I'd have meditated
So like an effigy I followed
Sitting on the now-itching cushion
Only to be animated on Niger Bridge
To see the symbolic demarcation
Of the south-east and west
While I thought we've arrived
With a glimpse of Idumota post-bridge

The driver settled another toll
My hope died inside me instantly
So I couldn't jubilate thereafter
When at Zik Avenue we stopped
To battle another exploitative plot
Which we waived with weariness
Emanating from exhausted humility

At last we got to Garki Park
To board bus to Agwu Camp
But the fare put at fifty naira in 1998
Suggested to me a new beginning
Then I decided to stay dumb
And when I saw another toll paid
I was the least amazed
Ignorant of even a flat tyre
That facilitated our inconveniences.
I got filled with silent curses
For the brain behind the scheme of
Now Your Suffering Continues.
But at last we alighted
My loads I couldn't carry
Drunk with fatigue and bitterness
But slightly happy for being off-road
To queue again for hours at sunset
To secure a non-existing hostel
Then I praised the unschooled
For taking the short cut to life arbitrary.
At last I was belatedly roomed
In a twelve-bed cubicle

In bond with complete aliens
A grace I nearly lost
Before other's plight I realized
In a five-hundred inmate's dormitory
With rage, tiredly I queued again for food
In the cold begging like confined inmates
But I was soon shown my fate
That I had no card for the meal
Upon which I became madly mad
Flying off the handle in earnest
An act that brought excess food supply.
At the sixth hour the next day
I was kitted for regimental fitness
Which reminded me my occupation
I made new allies and abstained
Innocently from my old pals
Enjoying the bitterness of orientation
I saw anxious ladies running after men
For fear of being termed, I don't even know…
Dubious men enjoyed the rush
I remember I got one too, under duress I may say
At least this National Slavery had some dividends.

The toilets were better if not existent
As I saw brimming toilet bowls for the first time
Practically with maggots feasting joyfully around
I had no choice but to add mine to the mount
Till I learnt the path to outdoor shot puts
For the first time I bathed in a populated open space.
I particularly loved the maami market

And various extracurricular activities
And the religious hypocrisy garnished with youthful zeal
The most intriguing part was the nights at the roundabouts
Seeing the sincere display of open shameless atrocities
Men and women reenacting the gory of Sodom

Just as we've adapted and the fun started flowing
The parades, relationships, mountaineering, among others
Behold the judgment day, I got a letter of deployment
I was sentenced with many
To one-year service imprisonment
With hard teaching labour in the remotest of places
I looked up to appeal the perceived injustice
Then I saw again the golden sub-section in my mind's eyes
To pay the supreme sacrifice
If need be, for the fatherland
And the appeal was quashed.

◄——— NOTE ———►

The poem starts with an account of the poet's experience as a new graduate, awaiting his deployment letter for the mandatory National Service, upon graduation. He was filled with so much excitements going to the eastern part of Nigeria, given the fact that he was not well travelled, and sees the opportunity to know new place beacons on him. Things turned sour when the journey became longer than expected, the road condition burdensome and the disappointment in the people he met in the course of the journey. He was happy seeing the Niger Bridge for the first time, and Onitsha with a semblance of Lagos Island, but his joy was cut short when he learnt that was just like half-way in the celebrated journey. He became so dejected that he wished he did not go to school. At the end, the joy of getting to the destination was one of mixed feelings as he had to queue for accommodation and food. To add sorrow to his agony, the living condition of the hostel was a big mess, and he also saw desperate ladies running against biological clock and being taken advantage of by men. In all, everyone adapted and enjoyed the episodes, but all was cut-off as the orientation ended and real service had to start.

43

AJUWAYAH II

It was a pleasing uniformed stress
Getting to Garki that June ending
En-route Ohaozara that night
Seated among shapeless luggage
And the frightening looking Jehu.
We headed towards our haven
Amid hamlets on gullied roads
Engulfed totally with dusty darkness
Disturbed by the children's compliments
From behind reed fences and bushy pavements
We tried to subject our piloting CLO
Into breath-taking interrogations
Which he beautifully answered
Employing diplomatic lies where necessary
Just to humanize our feelings.

Through the rays of the one-eyed headlamp
In front of the mobile warehouse brought to pick us
We saw nothing but illuminated bushes
And some jubilant bush creatures
Trying to impress and welcome us.
There were times we climbed
Delicate bridges whose noise
Is enough punishment for felonies
But we did not stop.

At another time we alighted
Forced to cross the bridge on foot
As the structure could not bare
The weight of passengers and bus at once.

When the journey persisted for two hours
We protested out of fear
To be briefed where the Eldorado lies
And we got another fantastic lie of comfort
And so we relaxed fearfully praying
Against serving otokoto's appetite.
We continued in accelerando for half hour
Then I appreciated Nigeria's wasteful size

At last, we alighted en masse
At Nkwo-Agu, Isu around the 21st hour
Inside the thick darkness that can ever be
And our legs a lifeless painful waste
Dangling like that of a little child's first steps
Our stomach, a deserted town.
We managed to greet our anxious hosts
Ndewoo, the only weapon we had
To break the language barrier
But came a belated surprising response
In a polished western tongue
Then our spirits rose instantaneously
Knowing there are people to converse with
The pains fading with the dawning joy
That soon showed us its slender body
When the eighteen of us dying of hybrid of pains
Were taken to the Onicha Local Government Canteen

To eat for the night were greeted by jubilant snakes
Then I doubted whether I will eventually serve Nigeria
As we met with four other corpers
That were there before us
All armed with jail-issued torch lights
We all shared the ills and goods of recent lives
A harrowing account of our pilgrimage.

At the canteen proper
I sat in amusing dilemma
When served with the only food available
A sliming vegetable, that left us with no choice
To refuse or receive to save my famished frame.
At last I ate and couldn't fathom
Why or how it tasted nice on my dried tongue
And resting well in my deserted stomach
As escorted by a mysterious cold Fanta
That tasted more like a concentrate than soft drink
We headed homeward to a place of rest
At the Copers' Lodge
We were divided into sleeping platoons
And deployed to different divisions.
The next day we're at the canteen again
Repeating our attack of previous night
Before we eventually journeyed
To our various places of assignments
Some to Oshiri, Abaomege and Ugulangu
Some to Ukawu, Isinkwo and Obiozara
While two of us went to Enuagwu
To commence a service
Of regrettable diligence.

That was where I begged my employer to reject me
When I saw that I couldn't survive the living conditions
I was to live in a house with no bathrooms
And when I insisted on one by all means
We're offered one on the third street
I was happy when rejected
That paved way for my transfer to
Oshiri Community Secondary School
Erikoro-ticha
I can never forget Principal C.N Obasi
Master of intrigues and strategies
As he fondly called himself
It was more of war than service
Until we humbled him with our Lagos sense.
I enjoyed the students and Mr. Apia though
Especially the sporting aspects
I officiated many football matches
Qualified the school for State Volleyballs competition
And won the trophy without playing any match
When NYSC came visiting, they realized
How much they'd suffered us
What we faced, serving our nation.

◄——— NOTE ———►

This is a sequel to the poem titled Ajuwayah, an account of the national
service proper. It narrates the experience from the point the poet
departed the orientation camp with others to Onicha Local
Government in Ebonyi State, Nigeria. It shows how bad the roads are,
the poor community and general scary moments bound to be
experienced by first time visitors.

44

OSHIRI ROADS

We are by no means profane please note
Though we gullied and never tasted tar
Deplorably non-functional and menacing
To automobiles and their owners.

It's so sad to behold what we have become
Our iridescent nature purpose from birth:
Alive as passage for Jehus and trekkers
But turned to ponds whenever it rains.

Come let me show you one of our greatest pitfalls
Your MPs and their ilk never came visiting
"Let 'em loose" they say,
'Cos we're plaguily producing sorrow

Not even any gutter on our hinges
When we weep, pee or poop
No wonder we became boreholes
From pitiable potholes.

But this is our fearsome concerns
Status quo shall remain
Wrapped in flowery manifestoes
Till oil comes out of our pores
And the high and mighty will adopt us
In their renown deft devious devilish design
Someday.

◄──── NOTE ────►

A direct personification of the roads at Oshiri, Onicha Local Government in Ebonyi State as at the time the poet was serving there as a youth corps member. It portrays the deplorable state of the roads with utter neglect by the MPs including those biologically related to the community. In conclusion, it hints on the hypocrisy of the politicians, who would be seen passionately claiming the area if tomorrow come, and oil is found there.

45

DEATH MUST DIE

Your constant cruel craze today unveiled
Armageddon my next parish of call
When your brutal escapades I sole-weighed
I will brandish my iron like a pal
Though chemical matters within I held
To get you unanimated with ill
For my inamorata and liefs tamed
Just before my dance at the market hall

Oh! You are not housed as me
For me to take challenge to
This man lives not within home
I've failed to weigh in toto
Your cruel fictitious real state
Folly! My arms not up to.

The writer, enraged with death, plans a revenge against death killing his
beloved family and friends and he will then go celebrate. Just then, it
dawn on him that death is a spirit, "you are not housed as me." He
therefore accepts his fate, sequel to a bad analysis of the planned battle.

46

TO THE SOLDIER HERO

Where are the khaki arbiters
Are they still in parliament?
Carpenters in the banking hall
Please hearken to my tidings:
If you persistently linger
You shall inanely litter
And in your quest for fame
You shall be cornered in shame.

We've pondered on our roles
We called our calabash dustbin
And you occupy it with dust
But judgement day has come
When we say it is enough
The band boys must halt the rhythm
Please change not the beat
Leave the scene.

◄——— NOTE ———►

A lampoon of military in politics, prevalent in Africa. It challenges the
military to return to the barracks, despite realizing that they came
because of the failure of the politicians in the first place- "Leave the
scene," "Please change not the beat"

47

LETTER TO MY ANGEL

Though taken away you are
From my sense of sight
Your genotype rests in my bosom
Nursing the root of my love
Please note this confessed assertion:
The wall of partition built with saliva
Shall be crippled by the dew
And the wall of Jericho
Falling beneath our feet
Shall be the desired steps
For us to move higher
Out of sight is long of heart

◄——— NOTE ———►

Here, the poet expresses his love to a lady he loves, whom he referred
to as Angel. It seems they have been separated by circumstances of life.
He however shows his hope as it declares that the present predicament
is temporary, that even with the distance between them comes a
growing fondness

48

LETTER TO MY ANGEL II

From whence came it?
I cannot really fathom
Except that like the wind
I enjoyed what the source
I could hardly comprehend
And out of the illusory experience
I confessed silently then
My invaluable love with passion
But now I can certainly confirm
That I lied in my throat.

Or why should I be this hypnotized
In talking about you
In singing about you
In dreaming about you
In praying about you
I eat when I assume you're
Sleep when I presumed you're
Do only things I envisage you're
Worse still, I live anticipating you're
Oh! This is beyond love's scope
Truly, I lied that I love you
I hope I'll not libate you
Against His will.

And again, this empirical observation:
You are never fashionable to me
Because you are never out of fashion
Oh! Where is the fountain of this
Classical immortality you possess
Thou unfair genius of loving escapades
Of invaluable role in my life's plot?

◄——— NOTE ———►

This is a sequel to the poem titled "Letter to my Angel". Here, the poet
buttresses the love expressed in the first part, wondering how he even
got to this height of love that makes him looks like one hypnotised

49

BEYOND THE TALENT

A lyrical soloist legend
With a voice of one-thousand
Keat's Nightingale in bond
Once found herself compete amid
Other gurus, so deep and celebrated.
A naïve girl by the side panicked
Upon seeing the stars ahead
And for help to one legend, she cried
And with compassion I saw our legend
Quickly consoled, groomed and encouraged
The girl, just for her to feel good and loved.
After all the gurus expected and respected finished
To the admiration of the audience, and judges amazed
With no expectation and for fun, somebody, the girl noted.
And to the girl, the judges sarcastically turned
Demanding that her special song be rendered
And our hurriedly tutored girl summoned
Her courage-within to deliver a unique, distilled
And memorable melody unprecedented
All in the hall surrendered and in awe-admiration stood
To appreciate the diamond from the mud, once despised
A rare product from the hasty school of our legend
Who with other stars before our girl, successfully failed.
Then it was evident it could only be God
And out of her inner-man a voice our girl heard:

"Your divine gift betters the job for which you trained,"
When your gifts and talents are developed and surrendered
To the One and only Potentate to be glorified.

NOTE

This is an account of how a little girl, competing in a singing
competition came out victorious, despite her initial fears, which caught
the attention of one of the superstars, favoured to win the
competition, that mentored her and encouraged her. This monorhyme
ends pastorally as it acknowledges the God-factor in such a situation,
concluding on the fact that divine gifts are better than your talent or
abilities earned from trainings, especially when developed and
surrendered for good use to glorify God.

50

UNPROVOKED ATTACK

Though I've known you for long
Astoundingly, our gap-between also long
In all manners of instinctive dispositions
    I shut my mouth

Though my lifetime yields I shared with you
Wrapped away are they in iron foil still by you
Cynically marveling at my no-resistance chicken strengths
    I shut my mouth

Though you made me grope inexorably
In an illuminated dark duel dishonourably
When on you I leaned in absolute trusts
    I shut my mouth

Though I groaned under your weight
Of comical humiliation all to your delight
You barked silently at my helpless groanings
    I shut my mouth

Though I saunter shamefully shamed
You stole my ingrained dignity charging aloud
My hope you amputated remorselessly in bales
    I shut my mouth

Though from your lustful heart to the eyes
You deprived me the princess of my loving escapades-
My sugary infatuated debut of reasonable humanities
       I shut my mouth

Though invisible by fate in my acts of forbearance
My noisy silence engulfed your guilt-inclined conscience
Even when life showered me favour in abundance
       I still solemnly shut my mouth

As my spirit became lifted brimming with praise
You languished in the harvest of your fruitful seeds
Now living life on my terms and in the Light's light
I wonder at the desperately wicked human heart
Spreading the Good News of doing well and doing good
       As He filled and opened my mouth.

NOTE

This is an emotional account of betrayal, not by an opposite sex, but a
friend of the poet, who even snatched his girlfriend, bullies him and
denied him many things till karma turns things around.

THE END

Author's Contact
Email: 247relevant@gmail.com

THE BOOK

"Echoes of Hope", is a profound collection of 50 poems encapsulating the essence of life as a young African. Through raw and heartfelt verses, the author shares a poignant account of personal growth, emotions, and aspirations spanning over three decades. From reflections on individual experiences to impassioned commentary on the political landscape of Africa, particularly Nigeria, each poem serves as a poetic diary, capturing the essence of life lessons and navigating the ever-evolving African political dramas. Within these pages lie didactic treasures, some fictional yet deeply impactful, aimed at instigating paradigm shifts and enhancing the readers' value system. 'Echoes of Hope' is more than just a collection of poems—it's a profound testament to the resilience of the human spirit and a beacon of hope for a brighter tomorrow.

The book is a journey with benefits:
- Pathfinder to Understanding Life. Gain insights and perspectives that illuminate the complexities of life, offering guidance and clarity in navigating its twists and turns.
- Exploration of Purpose. Delve into the subject of purpose, uncovering profound truths that inspire introspection and empower readers to discover their unique calling.
- Insights on Relationships. Explore the dynamics of relationships through the lens of poetry, gaining wisdom and understanding to cultivate meaningful connections with others.
- Making Meaningful Contributions. Discover how to impart and impact your world, as 'Echoes of Hope' inspires readers to actively engage in shaping a better future for themselves and their communities.

This book is a must read for everyone who wants to immerse themselves into a soul stirring journey of Self-discovery.

THE AUTHOR

Deji Atekoja, a dynamic force with a kaleidoscope of talents. With an MBA from the University of Technology Akure and expertise spanning from procurement to project management, he's a seasoned administrator and business development expert. A charismatic leader, he's pioneered numerous corporate initiatives in Nigeria and the United States. But his talents don't stop there—he's also a social commentator, writer, artistic director, and teacher. Known for his strategic thinking and love for rhymes, he's a husband to an author, father to budding poetic singers, and a creative mind with a knack for typographic design and film composition. Get ready to be inspired by his multifaceted journey!

9 798322 534365